Congratul...

Hillcroft Primary School
Hill Croft, HC2 3PS

8th July

Dear Class 1,

Thank you for inviting us to see your play. I thought it was very good. I really liked the song at the end. I did not know the story. Did you make it up yourselves?

How did you make the masks? They looked very real. The monkeys were funny and the elephants' trunks were brilliant.

Well done! You were great!

From,

Ben Brown

Thank You for a Birthday Present

15 Silver Street
Ashton
AS2 9GQ

5th May

Dear Aunty Pat,

Thank you very much for the torch you sent me for my birthday. It is very useful. I like using it in the garden at night to see if the foxes have come. I like flashing it on and off to send messages. I like using it to read in bed after Dad has turned out the light. Don't tell him!

Last Saturday Dad took me and three of my friends to the zoo for my birthday. I liked watching the apes and the big cats best. One of the chimps had a new baby. She was holding it in her arms for ages. I still want to be a zoo vet or work in a wildlife park when I grow up.

I hope we can come and stay with you soon. Then I can help look after the ducks and the hens. How is Minty? I can't wait to see her and her new kittens. I am going to ask Dad if I can have one.

Lots of love,

Alex

Holiday Letter

Hotel Bianca
12th June

Dear Class 3,

Hello everyone! I am having a brilliant time in Spain. I go swimming every day. The sun is hot and I've made lots of new friends!

I love it here in Spain, but there are some things that are not so good:

1. There are too many mosquitoes. I've been bitten ten times so far.

2. The sand is too hot. You can't walk on it.

3. I can't get to sleep at night because it is so hot.

I've never been to Spain before so these things are new to me.

I've joined a club for two weeks. We play lots of games and have lots of competitions. The BEST competition so far was the one with

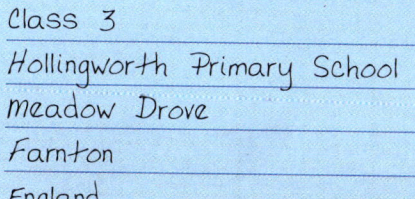

Class 3
Hollingworth Primary School
Meadow Drove
Farnton
England

water pistols. We had to see who could shoot the water the farthest. A boy called Adam won.

I haven't told you about our hotel. It looked OK from the outside. Inside it was HORRIBLE! We thought the one nice thing about the hotel was the beds. But as soon as we put our heads on the pillows, YUCK! They smelt horrible. We went to see the Holiday Rep. She put us in a much better hotel. It is lovely. We have got two big rooms for half price!

See you soon. I'll be back next week.

      Kelly

Get Well Soon

36 Barton Street
Barton
BT18 4AZ

27th April

Dear Pippa,

I am very sorry that you are in hospital. I hope you get better soon. There are lots of things that I want to do with you. We could watch some videos. I have got three new ones.

I've been doing lots of things while you have been in hospital. This is one of them: I've been to Anna's birthday party. It was brilliant! We went bowling, then to McDonald's, then we had a sleepover.

Oh, I almost forgot! We have got a rabbit. I have called him Flopsy. He is very cute and cuddly! I get to look after him.

I hope the hospital beds are comfy. Have you made any friends in hospital?

Get well soon. I miss you.

From your good friend,

Abby   xoxoxxoxx

Thank You for Having Me

20 Hayes Road
Park End
PK10 8HR

16th March

Dear Grandpa,

Thank you very much for the lovely visit to your house. I had a really good time. The dinner you cooked was the best I have ever tasted! I always like roast dinners and I love trifle. I hope I will be able to cook like you when I am older.

Children's Letters

by Julie Garnett

Contents

Section 1
Request for Help to Parents	2
Congratulations to Class 1	3
Thank You for a Birthday Present	4
Holiday Letter	6
Get Well Soon	8
Thank You for Having Me	10

Section 2
Pen Pal	12
Thank You to Visiting Performers	15
Suggestion to the School Council	18
Letter to an Editor: Personal Opinion	20
Complaint About Traffic	22

Section 3
Thank You and Newsletter to Nan	24
Complaint to a Bike Shop	28
Complaint About an Accident	31

Edinburgh Gate
Harlow, Essex

Request for Help to Parents

Hillcroft Primary School
Hill Croft, HC2 3PS

26th April

Dear Parents,

Please can you help us? We are making a wildlife pond and we need some help.

There are two ways you can help.

1. You can help us dig out the pond. Can you give us some time next Saturday?

2. We will need plants for the pond. Have you got some that you can let us have?

Please let Mrs Patel know if you can help.

From,

Class 3

Can you come and have dinner with us soon? I could try to make one of those trifles. It's a good job I wrote down how to make it. I'll talk to Mum about it and hope she says yes.

Thank you again for having me. It was great to see you.

Lots of love,

Rosie

Pen Pal

15 Park Close
Bridgeford
BF12 0PC

10th June

Dear Emma,

I couldn't wait to write to you for the first time! I have never had a pen pal before, so I am really looking forward to getting to know you. But first let me tell you about myself.

I am eight years old and my full name is Katie Ann James. I have short brown hair and I am quite tall for my age. I go to Wayland Primary School and I am in 3B, Mr Garland's class.

In my family there is my mum, my dad and me. As I am an only child I sometimes get bored at home — so I keep very busy with lots of hobbies.

- 2 -

My main ones at the moment are art, gym, dance and drama.

Let me tell you about what's been happening over the last few months. In April I joined a drama group called Starlight Dance and Theatre Company. Six of us were chosen to audition for a TV programme. It was really exciting. We went to the television studios and had to act in front of some people. Unfortunately we didn't get another phone call, but I was thrilled to have taken part. Maybe I will have another chance another day! As I expect you can tell, I would love to be an actor.

I love going to the theatre as well. I have been to the London Palladium and Her Majesty's Theatre. Every year Mum and Dad take me to a pantomime.

- 3 -

Now I have told you a little bit about me, please write and tell me about yourself soon.

Looking forward to hearing from you,

Best wishes,   Katie James

Thank You to Visiting Performers

Meadway Junior School

Birlington Lane
Birlington
BT9 2MS

10th March

Dear Laser Dynamics,

Thank you for coming to our school and putting on a laser show for us. I enjoyed it a lot.

It was fun learning how to remember the colours of the rainbow and what the word 'laser' means. I'm sending you what I've done.

The lasers were brilliant, especially the animals walking on the ceiling. I'd love to see them again. Thank you for making it so interesting. I hope you can come back and put on another show for us.

From

Ben Pitts

LASER

Light
Amplification
by
Stimulated
Emission
of
Radiation

COLOURS OF THE RAINBOW

Red	Richard
Orange	Of
Yellow	York
Green	Gave
Blue	Battle
Indigo	In
Violet	Vain

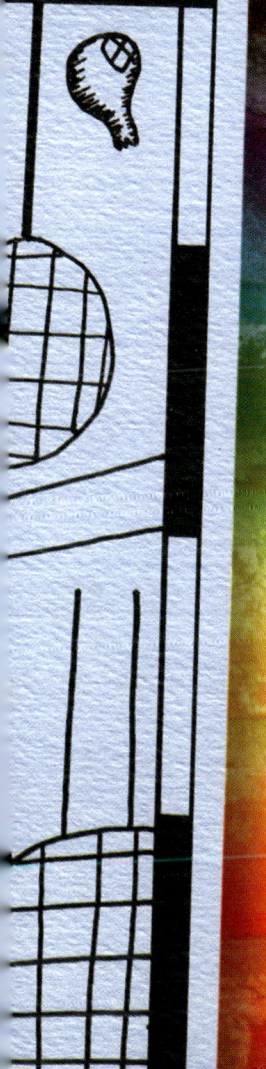

Suggestion to the School Council

Wayland Primary School

Stockwood Close
Stockwood

Dear School Council,

I am writing to point out the problem children have if they want to go to two clubs that are held at the same time. For example, Netball Club and Rugby Club are both held after school on Tuesdays.

If one club could be moved to a lunchtime, this would solve the problem of a clash. I think it would be better to move netball rather than rugby. Children don't get so dirty playing netball and they can get ready for afternoon school more quickly.

The present situation is very disappointing for children like me who enjoy sport and want to join as many clubs as possible.

Please would you consider my idea?

Thank you.

David Green

Letter to an Editor: Personal Opinion

8 South Drive
Eastley
ES14 3SD

18th June

Dear Editor,

I am writing in reply to the article in your newspaper dated June 13th about the collie dog found wandering on the M5. I was ashamed of whoever threw that poor puppy out of a car.

How could anyone do that? Everyone should remember that a dog is for life not just for Christmas, wrapped in pretty bows and ribbons. I feel so sorry for this poor unwanted dog.

I hope this is the last case of cruelty to animals. I would like a dog and would never do such a horrid thing. I was very glad to read that little Lilly has found a new home that can give her the love and care she needs.

Kirstie Darling

Lilly

PS: Dogs have feelings, too. Please don't hurt them.

Complaint About Traffic

250 Holloway Road
Stockwood
SW3 7HR

30th June

Dear Sir or Madam,

I am writing to you as I am concerned about the amount of traffic and parking outside the shops in Holloway Road.

The main problem happens around 8.45am and 3.00pm. Both these times are when children are going to or coming home from school. Cars speed along Holloway Road, making it dangerous for children to cross on their own.

Secondly, the old people who live in the flats across the road from the shops also find it difficult to cross the road.

I would like to point out that we only have one crossing in the area and this is on the main road, not on the busy Holloway Road. Would it be possible to have a crossing by the shops in Holloway Road? This would make it safer for children and old people.

Yours faithfully,

Suzanne Brooks

Thank You and Newsletter to Nan

2 Fern Bank Avenue
Fern Bank
Bristol

6th January

Dear Nan,

Do you realise I haven't written to you since November and it is January now, a new year? I am writing to tell you what I have been doing over the last two months. Before I do, I would just like to check that you are well. I am doing nicely, apart from a nasty knock on my knee – yes, you guessed it - from playing football!

I'll start with Christmas. I had lots of wonderful presents, the best of which was yours! Thank you ever so much; no one else had the good idea of taking me on holiday. I'm really looking forward to spending the summer with you in the sun. Recently the place where we will be staying was on television. Did you see it? It looked great, especially the swimming pool.

Other presents I received include: a LOT of chocolate, new trainers and pyjamas. I also had a scooter which I have been playing on recently, but not as much as I wanted to because of the awful weather!

Now some news about the rest of the family. We'll start with Joe, my mischievous brother. Over the last few weeks he has been more active than usual! The other day he broke one of Mum's favourite ornaments. He should have known better than to kick a football around the house, especially in Mum's bedroom! (He got the football with a Kid's Meal from the fish and chip shop.)

Nothing different has been happening with Dad. He's his old self: eating crisps, lazing about watching TV – and going to work now and again!

Mum is OK. She has just recovered from a heavy cold that spoilt her New Year as she couldn't go to any parties.

Finally me. At school I have joined the gym club where we use the vault and have learned some exciting moves. In the holidays I visited Baskerville's gym club where I was coached by a man who has entered the Olympic Games. It was hard at first but I soon improved and coped with the strain!

Well, I have got to sign off now as my friend has just arrived to sleep for the night. Thanks again for the brilliant present.

Lots of love,
Jack

Complaint to a Bike Shop

Upper Church Street
Sandwell Green
Welling
WL12 9SG

12th August

Dear Sir,

I recently bought a bike from your store. I had been saving for a long time to purchase this particular bike because of its good reputation and many features. One of the main reasons I chose this model was because of its dual suspension system. However, when it was delivered, the suspension was very stiff. At first I thought this was because the bike was new and needed to be worn in. When I tried to adjust the suspension I realised that you couldn't, even though your leaflets said you could.

How can customers trust your advertising if things you publish are false? Moreover, what do you suggest I do about my bike which behaves as if it has no suspension at all?

I suggest the options open to you are:
- Repair the bike within ten days.
- Replace the bike.
- Give me a full refund.

Unless I have a satisfactory response, it is highly unlikely that I will use your store in the future. Furthermore, I will not recommend your store to other people.

I await a speedy reply.

Yours faithfully,

Will North

Complaint About an Accident

26 Beech Avenue
Stockwood

4th May

Dear City Council,

I am writing to express my concerns about the roadworks in Ladman Road, Stockwood.

On Saturday 15th December, I was riding my bike up Ladman Road when suddenly my front wheel went into a hole in the road, which made me fall off my bike and land awkwardly on my arm. Fortunately, a neighbour saw me, called an ambulance and informed my parents who went with me to the hospital in the ambulance. My arm was X-rayed. It was broken and had to be put in plaster. This was not much fun as I was unable to ride my bike or my new scooter for some time.

If the hole in the road had been filled in immediately after it appeared, my accident would not have happened. As it is still there, I suggest that you arrange for it to be repaired, otherwise another cyclist might have an accident and could be seriously injured if another vehicle came along at the same time.

The road workers originally dug up the road at the end of March. I am sure you will agree it is about time they finished it.

I look forward to hearing from you.

Yours faithfully,

Lucy Humphries